🐾 Why do animals have spots?

Cats, including leopards and jaguars have spots for camouflage. They hide in the trees to sleep or watch their prey. The light through the leaves makes everything look spotted, so their spotty coats mean that other animals can't see them.

![Discovery Kids logo] DISCOVERY KIDS™

Why do animals have tails?

PaRragon

Bath · New York · Singapore · Hong Kong · Cologne · Delhi
Melbourne · Amsterdam · Johannesburg · Auckland · Shenzhen

Acknowledgements:
Photo credits: b = bottom, t = top, r = right, l= left, m= middle
Front cover: ©Terry Carr | Dreamstime.com, back cover images iStockphoto
All internal images: iStockphoto, except p4: b © Marcin Ciesielski / Sylwia Cisek | Dreamstime.com, p10: b Gettyimages, p12: tr Gettyimages, p13: m Gettyimages, p18: t © Robert Gubiani | Dreamstime.com, b © Khudoberdina Asiya | Dreamstime.com, p20: t © Trevor Kelly | Dreamstime.com, p21: t Gettyimages, p24: t Gettyimages, p26: t Gettyimages, b Gettyimages, p30: tl Gettyimages, bl Gettyimages, p31: b Gettyimages, p36: t Gettyimages, p37: t Gettyimages, b Gettyimages, p41: br Gettyimages, poster: front br Shutterstock.

First published by Parragon in 2011

Parragon
Queen Street House
4 Queen Street
Bath BA1 1HE, UK

Copyright © Parragon Books Ltd 2011

ISBN 978-1-4454-5946-2

Printed in China

CONTENTS

INVERTEBRATES

🐾 Which animals are spineless?

About 90 percent of all the animals on Earth have no backbone, or spine. They are called invertebrates and range from snails to big, wobbly jellyfish. All invertebrates are cold-blooded—their body temperature is the same as the air or water around them.

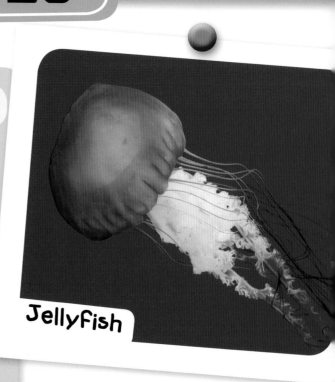

Jellyfish

🐾 Which is the biggest boneless creature?

The biggest invertebrate is the giant squid, with a 26 foot (8 m) long body and even longer tentacles. It lives in the ocean, where the water supports its weight.

Snail

Oyster

Snails and oysters are closely related. They both belong to a family of animals known as mollusks. Snails and Oysters have soft bodies and shells.

🐾 **Do worms have a skeleton?**

Earthworm

Earthworms are invertebrates—they do not have a spine or any other bones. But they do have water-filled tubes, which run along the length of their bodies and act a bit like a skeleton.

TEAMWORK

🐾 Why do fish go to school?

Lots of fish swim together in groups called schools. There's safety in numbers, and individuals are less likely to be picked off by hungry hunters, such as sharks.

School of fish

🐾 Where would you find a town of dogs?

Prairie dogs are a type of rodent, relatives of mice and rats, that live in the U.S. and Mexico. Millions may live together in underground "towns."

Prairie dogs

Beavers work together to build dams. They use young trees to dam rivers and make mini lakes. They store young trees in the lake for them to eat later!

Beaver cutting down tree

Which insects are champion builders?

In relation to their size, termites work together and build bigger structures than any other creature. They use grains of soil as bricks, and their own spit as cement.

Termites

KEEPING CLEAN

🐾 Who bathes in dirt?

Zebras and horses love to take a dirt bath. The grit works through their hair and rubs off any dead skin, while the dust soaks up oil from their coat. Lots of other furry creatures take dirt baths, too, including cats and dogs.

Zebra

🐾 Which fish goes to the cleaners?

The grouper fish that lives on coral reefs goes to a special cleaning station when it wants to get spruced up. Shrimps and tiny fish called wrasse clean the grouper by eating up any lice, fungus, or dead skin.

Grouper fish

Oxpecker

🐾 Who lends a helping beak?

Oxpeckers (African birds) help pick ticks (insects) off a rhino's face. The rhino sits very still, even when the birds' sharp beaks are poking around its eyes and nostrils. It works out well for everyone—the rhino gets rid of the itchy ticks, and the oxpeckers get a free meal.

DISCOVERY FACT™

A cat's tongue is covered with tiny spines, which it uses to comb its fur to keep it nice and clean.

COMMUNICATING

Who dances for a mate?

A tree frog in Malaysia dances to attract his mate. The female can't see the dance, but she senses the movement of air as the male taps his feet.

Tree frog

Blue whale

Which is the loudest animal on Earth?

The blue whale is the biggest living animal, and also the loudest. It can send messages to other blue whales that are more than 310 miles (500 km) away!

Rattlesnake

Burrowing owl

Rattlesnakes are not the only animal to "rattle." Burrowing owls do, too. They rattle so they sound dangerous, like rattlesnakes, to scare predators.

Which animal breathes in Morse code?

Morse is a secret code made by mixtures of short and long signals. Rhinos seem to use a similar system to talk to each other. They string together special mixes of short and long breaths!

CAMOUFLAGE

Which lizard looks like a tree trunk?

The leaf-tailed gecko's speckled skin blends in perfectly with the trunk of a tree. So long as this reptile keeps still, its clever camouflage stops any predator from noticing it.

Leaf-tailed gecko

Why are zebras stripy?

Black and white stripes confuse lions and other predators. The stripes seem to wobble in the heat haze. Each zebra has its own pattern, so stripes might also help a foal to find its mom in the herd.

Butterflies have eyes on their wings but not for seeing with. They're spots that look like eyes, to scare off predators.

Arctic hares

🐾 **Who wears two fur coats?**

Some mammals change their coat to match the season, including the hares, foxes, and wolves of the snowy north. Their brown coat turns white in winter for camouflage against the snow. It also grows extra-thick to keep out the cold.

Arctic fox

WEIRD WILD

🐾 Who gift-wraps dung?

Male dung beetles have a funny idea of what to give their girlfriend as a present – dung, to lay her eggs in. When the grubs hatch, they enjoy a smelly feast!

Dung beetle

🐾 Who gives drink cans to a mate?

The male kea displays red objects to impress his mate. He uses red flowers, buttons, or even cola cans!

Reindeer

Firefly

Male fireflies make their bottoms flash on and off with a glowing green light, like a beacon (torch) to impress the females.

Who locks horns for a mate?

Lots of male animals fight over females. It's a way of showing off and also means that only the strongest get to mate. Reindeer fight by locking horns and pushing—that way, their bodies are less likely to get badly hurt.

AMPHIBIANS

How can you tell a frog from a toad?

Most frogs have smooth skin, but toads are warty! Frogs and toads are the only amphibians that lose their tail and grow strong back legs for jumping.

Toad

Frog

Why are frogs slimy?

A frog's thin, slimy skin allows it to absorb oxygen from both air and water. Frogs are amphibians, animals that start life in water, but gradually change so they can survive on land, too.

🐾 Which is the weirdest amphibian?

The axolotl never really grows up! It breeds when it is still at "tadpole" stage and only changes into an adult body if its pond dries up and it is forced to live on land.

Axolotl

DISCOVERY FACT™

The goliath frog is the biggest frog, but the Chinese giant salamander is nearly four times as long.

AMAZING SIGHTS!

Echidna

Who plays follow-the-leader?

When it is time for a female echidna to mate, hopeful males line up to be chosen! Up to ten male echidnas follow her, nose-to-tail.

Where can you see more than a million crabs?

Every year, on Christmas Island in the Indian Ocean, millions of land crabs gather on the beach to lay their eggs. Each crab lays about 100,000 eggs!

Land crabs

When do seals come ashore?

Although seals spend all their life in the sea, they come ashore to have babies. The seals leave their babies after a few weeks, though, because there's nothing for the adult seals to eat on the beach.

Black widow spider

Many female spiders eat their mate. The meal gives her energy for making eggs.

PARENTING

Crocodile with young

🐾 Who rides in a crocodile's smile?

Female crocodiles are very gentle moms. They carry their babies down to the river in their mouth—being careful not to bite them!

🐾 Who leaves their babies with a babysitter?

Meerkats live together in large groups, or colonies. All the adults go out hunting during the day, leaving their babies in a nursery. One or two young adults are left behind to keep an eye on the little ones.

Malleefowl

Which bird cooks its own eggs?

The malleefowl buries its eggs under an enormous pile of sand. The anxious dad keeps adding or taking away the sand so the eggs stay at a steady, toasty temperature.

DISCOVERY FACT™

Adult elephants in a herd thump any badly behaved baby elephants with their trunks.

BIRDS

Parrots

Why do birds have feathers?

Soft, downy feathers keep birds' bodies toasty and warm, while waxy outer ones keep off the rain. Most importantly, feathers allow birds to fly. Birds beat their feathered wings to lift off the ground and fly through the air.

Why do eagles have such hooked beaks?

An eagle's hooked beak is perfect for tearing up meat. Herons have long beaks for spearing fish. Macaws have powerful beaks for cracking nuts.

Bald eagle

Can all birds swim?

No, but some can.
Penguins have
webbed feet,
stubby wings,
oily waterproof feathers
and a layer of fat to
keep them warm.

Penguins

DISCOVERY FACT™

Hummingbirds are the only
birds that fly backward. It
helps them to hover around
a flower filled with nectar.

Hummingbird

BABIES

Tree frog eggs

🐾 **Do tree frogs lay eggs in trees?**

Like all frogs, tiny tree frogs need to lay their eggs in water. They use pools of rainwater cupped in the leaves of rain-forest trees. There's fresh rain every day, so there's little danger of the eggs drying out.

🐾 **Which bird lays the biggest egg?**

The biggest bird lays the biggest egg! An ostrich is much taller than an adult human, and its eggs are giant, too. A single ostrich egg weighs more than 22 chicken eggs!

Ostrich

Do turtles lay eggs in the sea?

Turtles spend all their lives out at sea, but the moms come ashore to lay their leathery eggs. When the eggs hatch, the baby turtles crawl out of the sand and head straight down to the water.

Baby turtle

Cichlid

DISCOVERY FACT™

Some fish keep their eggs in their mouths. Eggs left alone to hatch are often eaten by other animals. Cichlids keep their eggs safe and sound in their mouths.

FAST ASLEEP

Where *do dormice* go in the winter?

In the fall, dormice are busy feeding on nuts and berries. That's because they spend the winter underground, in nests. A lining of dry grass and leaves makes the nest soft and snug.

Dormouse

Can birds sleep as they fly?

Swifts sometimes stay in the air for up to four years at a time, without ever landing. They don't just sleep in the air—they can drink, eat insects, and mate too!

Swifts

🐾 Who digs in for winter?

Bears sleep through the cold winter months, so they dig dens or stay in a cozy cave. They don't come out until the spring.

DISCOVERY FACT™

Animals have dreams when they sleep. Look at a pet cat when it's asleep. If its whiskers are twitching, it's probably dreaming about catching a mouse!

SPECIAL SENSES

Pit viper

🐾 Who hunts by heat?

The pit viper has an extra-special sense—it can detect heat. This helps it to find even the tiniest, best-hidden prey.

Bat

🐾 Can bats see in the dark?

No, bats use sound, not sight, to find their way at night. The noise of their screeches bounces off objects so the bats can figure out where they are, and what's around them.

Who has a built-in compass?

Monarch butterflies are the long-distance flight champions of the insect world. No one is certain how they find their way, but their bodies contain magnets, like a real compass.

DISCOVERY FACT™

Bats are not the only animals to use sound to find their way. Whales and dolphins use echoes to avoid bumping into things. This is called sonar— and submarines also use it!

Dolphin

HUNTING TRICKS

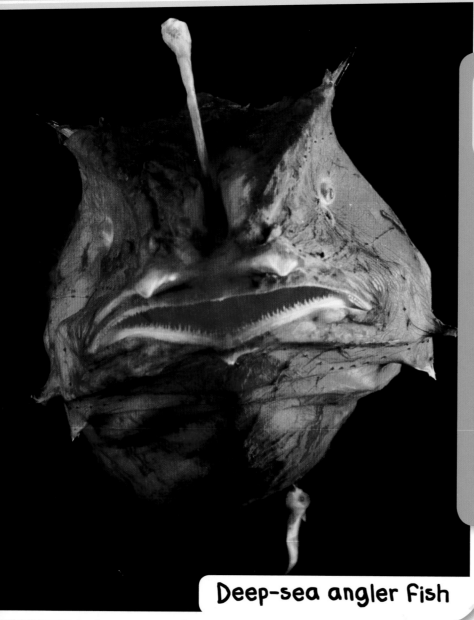

Deep-sea angler fish

🐾 Who goes fishing at the bottom of the sea?

The deep-sea angler fish feeds on other smaller fish, but it doesn't waste time and energy chasing them. Instead, it has a "fishing rod" to lure fish close to its mouth. It is very gloomy in the deep, so the "rod" glows in the dark.

DISCOVERY FACT™

The end of the death adder's tail looks like a juicy worm. When a bird flies down for it, the adder gobbles it up!

Stoat

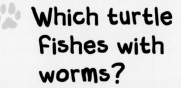 Why do animals have tails?

Most animals use their tails for balance when they are moving and jumping to help catch their prey. Cats and dogs use their tails to communicate with each other. Fish use their tails like propellers to move through the water and birds use them to help them fly.

Alligator snapping turtle

Which turtle fishes with worms?

The alligator snapping turtle has two fake "worms" on the tip of its tongue. It wiggles the worms to tempt hungry fish to come near—and when they do, it gulps them down!

REPTILES

🐾 Which animals have scaly skin?

Snakes, lizards, crocodiles, and turtles have dry, scaly skin. These cold-blooded creatures belong to a family of animals called reptiles. There are about 6,000 types of reptile.

Giant tortoise

🐾 How long do tortoises live?

Tortoises are the longest-living animals on Earth. Some probably live beyond their 200th birthday! Perhaps it's because their tough, bony shell protects them from dangerous predators.

Crocodile

Snakes can't blink, because they don't have any eyelids! A see-through scale protects each of their eyes.

🐾 How can you tell a crocodile from an alligator?

You can tell them apart by their smile. When a crocodile's mouth is shut, you can still see one of its bottom teeth poking out.

Alligator

33

EATING HABITS

Why do ants keep creepy-crawlies?

Ants look after herds of aphids just as farmers keep dairy cows! The sweet-toothed ants "milk" the aphids for the sugary liquid they produce.

Ants with aphids

Killer whale

What animal plays with its food?

Killer whales play with seal pups before they eat them. No one knows why they toss the pups into the air. It could be to stun them, or it could just be for fun.

Who is the fussiest eater?

The koala must be the fussiest creature on the planet. It will only eat eucalyptus, and sometimes it is so picky that it will only eat leaves from a particular tree!

Spider silk is super-strong, and also very sticky. Webs have caught mice and even small birds!

Koala

SELF DEFENSE

Which crab packs a stinging punch?

Everyone knows that anemones sting, including the clever boxer crab. He holds an anemone in his two front pincers and soon scares off his enemies!

Boxer crab

Which caterpillar turns into a snake?

One type of hawkmoth caterpillar makes itself look just like a tree snake when danger threatens. It shortens and thickens its head and turns over to reveal unblinking, snaky "eyes." It even has a flickering "tongue" to complete the scary disguise!

Hawkmoth caterpillar

Which beetle squirts poisonous gas?

The bombardier beetle uses poison to frighten away would-be attackers. It squirts a jet of hot, toxic liquid out of its bottom! The jet makes a noise like a gun being fired.

Bombardier beetle

Hawk eagle

DISCOVERY FACT™

The hawk eagle has a crest of feathers that stand up, so the bird seems bigger and scarier than it really is.

CRUSTACEANS

What kind of animal is a lobster?

The lobster is a type of invertebrate called a crustacean. Crustaceans have shells (crusts) and lots of jointed legs. A lobster has five pairs of legs, with claws on its front ones to grip and stab prey.

Lobster

Batwing coral crab

Who wears armor at the bottom of the sea?

The tough outer shell of a lobster or crab is like a suit of armor, stopping hungry fish and other predators from biting the animal's body. Most crabs live on the seabed, eating rotting remains that sink down there.

Hermit crab

DISCOVERY FACT™

Hermit crabs don't grow their own shells. They find an old, empty shell and hide their long, soft body in there instead!

How do crabs grow bigger?

Our skin stretches as we grow, but a hard shell can't stretch. When a crab grows too big for its shell, it gets rid of it. The new shell underneath is soft at first, but soon hardens. A crab can do this up to 20 times in its life.

INTELLIGENCE

Are dolphins as smart as us?

Dolphins seem to talk to each other, and they learn tricks really easily, but humans are still the cleverest species on Earth. We've learned how to read, write, build skyscrapers, and do many other complicated things.

Crow

Clever crows often carry nuts in their beaks until they are flying over a hard surface, such as concrete. They drop the nut so that its shell smashes, and swoop down to gobble up the insides.

🐾 **Who has a favorite stick?**

Chimps love to snack on crunchy termites, but their fingers are too short to pry them from their mound. Instead, the brainy chimps carry a stick to use like a fishing rod.

Chimpanzee

DANGEROUS!

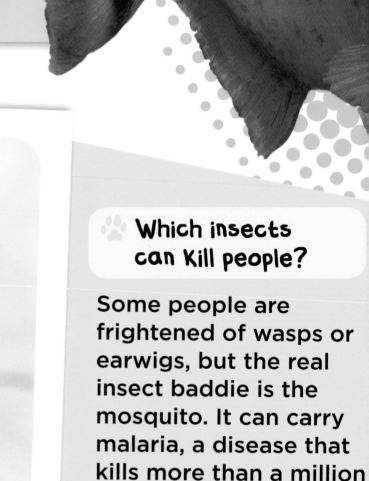

Piranha

Which are the scariest fish?

Sharks are the scariest fish in the sea, but the scariest river fish are piranhas. Piranhas have rows of razor-sharp teeth and can strip a body down to bare bone in seconds.

Mosquito

Which insects can kill people?

Some people are frightened of wasps or earwigs, but the real insect baddie is the mosquito. It can carry malaria, a disease that kills more than a million people each year.

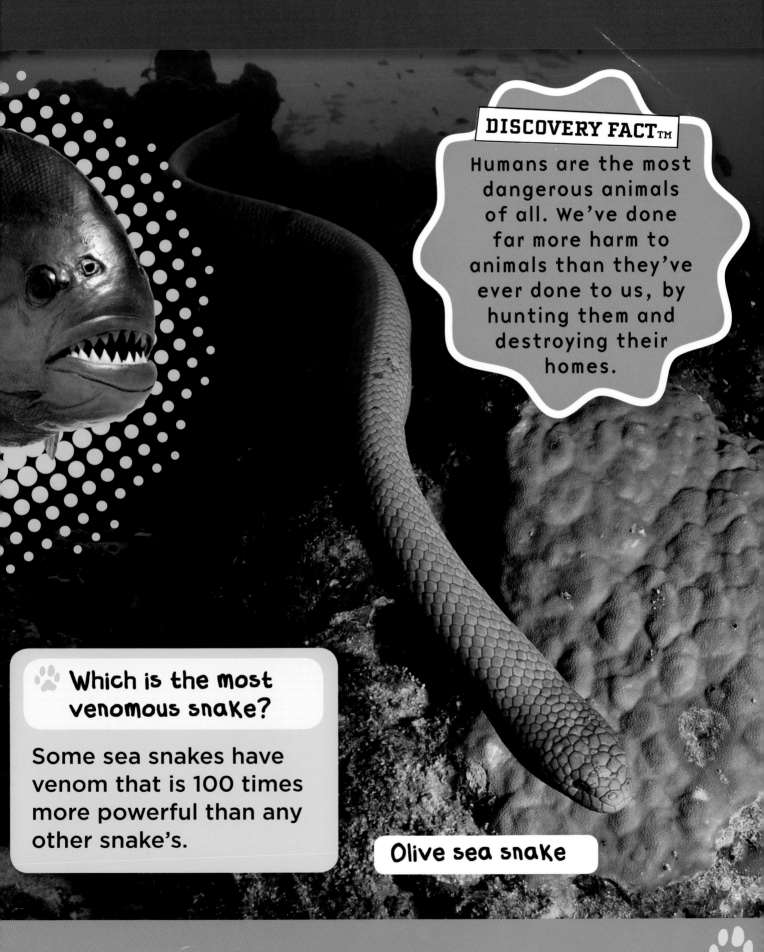

Humans are the most dangerous animals of all. We've done far more harm to animals than they've ever done to us, by hunting them and destroying their homes.

🐾 **Which is the most venomous snake?**

Some sea snakes have venom that is 100 times more powerful than any other snake's.

Olive sea snake

AMAZING FISH

Goldfish

How do fish breathe?

Fish have slits called gills on the sides of their heads, which allow them to get oxygen from water, just as we get oxygen from air. All fish breathe using gills.

DISCOVERY FACT™

Whales and dolphins are warm-blooded mammals, which come up for air. Fish are cold-blooded and breathe underwater.

How do salmon leap?

Salmon leap if they meet a mini waterfall when they are heading up river to breed. The strong, muscly tails that they use for swimming also help to thrust them up into the air.

Whale shark

Which fish would fit on your fingertip?

The dwarf goby is the tiniest fish in the world, at about half an inch (1 cm) long. The whale shark is biggest—it's about 40 ft (12 m) long from nose to tail, but quite harmless to people.

MAN'S BEST FRIENDS

🐾 When did cats move in with people?

Cats first became tame in Ancient Egyptian times. They were wildcats, who came to hunt mice and rats living in the grain supplies. The Egyptians were so grateful that they even worshiped a cat goddess!

Cowboy riding his horse

🐾 Why do cowboys ride horses?

People have ridden horses for thousands of years, in order to travel over huge stretches of land. Cowboys and gauchos ride so they can check on their cattle.